Life and Love

Takes us places we never thought we would go and
experience things we never thought we could stand

Stacey Anderson I

BK Royston Publishing
P. O. Box 4321
Jeffersonville, IN 47131
502-802-5385
http://www.bkroystonpublishing.com
bkroystonpublishing@gmail.com

© Copyright – 2019

All Rights Reserved. No part of this book may be reproduced, stored in a retrieval system, or transmitted by any means without the written permission of the author.

Cover Design Layout: Elite Covers
Front Cover Photo Credit: Roger Kirby
Back Cover Photo Credit: Carey Payne

ISBN-13: 978-1-951941-03-1

Printed in the United States of America

Dedication

This book is dedicated to my mother, Sandra J. Anderson and to my family and friends and everyone who realizes,

"Everything in Life is a Test."

Table of Contents

Dedication	iii
Introduction	vii
Transparent	2
Imagine	4
Just Love	6
My Life	8
Father	10
Time to Leave	12
Time to Leave Part 2	14
Pride	16
Lord Help	18
Reality	20
Trust	22
God Is	24

Do You Know	26
Please Lord	28
Peace	30
Release	32
Frienemy	34
More Peace	36
Safe	38
Comfortable	40
How Excellent	42
New	44
Never Settle	46
Change	48
Until Next Time	50

Introduction

There are many books today that are focused on uplifting and empowerment. However, this book is strictly to provide some encouragement while traveling through this thing called life. Life has a way of handling us with sometimes a reckless abandon.

My hope in sharing my thoughts would be that you would find comfort understanding that all of us have faced similar issues when it comes to Love and Life, but we Survived.

Stacey Anderson I

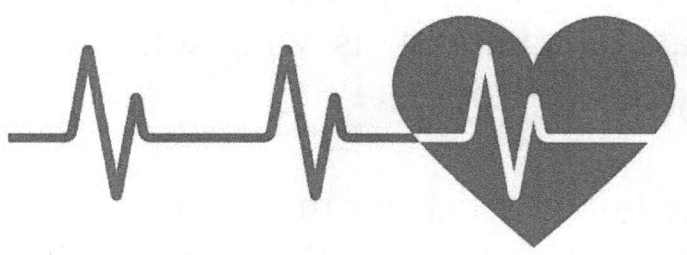

Transparent

Do you care that your words
in a text leave him unaware
Does it matter when clarity
is not clear
Will you change to show you
care
Will you have his back to let
him know you are there
That's the moment you
realize its
Love that you Share

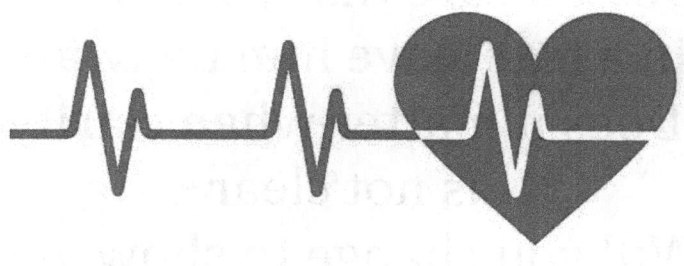

Imagine

Imagine not being able to let go.
How could you ever say no to his
beckoning of your touch
How would you know when you have
given enough
Is there a limit on how much you give
Or do you give all that you have
inside
So, he knows your eternal Love for
him you cannot hide
Imagine a feeling so overwhelming
that it makes it difficult to catch your
breath
So overwhelming that you feel close
to death
And then the Emotion reveals itself
And says, "I AM LOVE"

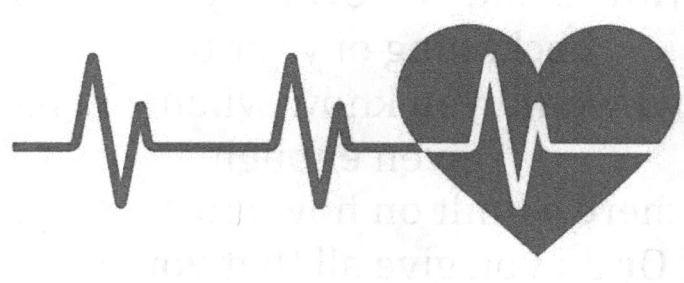

Just Love

Love without constraints,
Without guilt or concerns
There is no Emotion stronger
than Love
Love overpowers hate
Love with passion,
Love intentionally
Love until it hurts
Love until it works
Love until it brightens your day
Let Love lead the way
Where Love leads the Heart will
stay

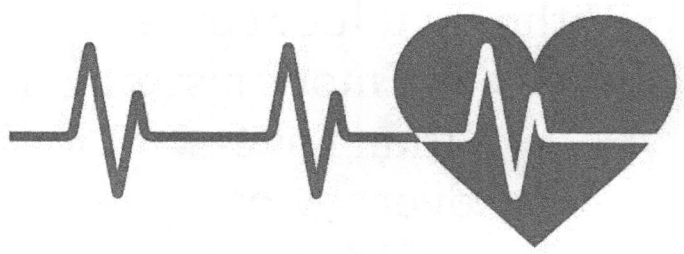

My Life

My Life without you is
a sad state of affairs

It would be so much
better

If my last name you
would wear

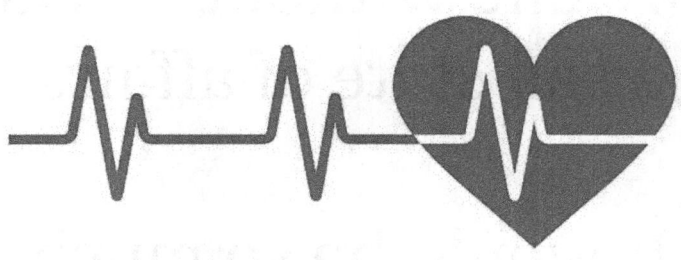

Father

Father can you help
I need to know what to do
When I cannot understand
How you move like you do
I want to know how to be like you
My Faith has been tested and
I am feeling weak
Father it is your grace and mercy
that I seek
My heart has been broken and
I am feeling crushed
Father I need you to lift me up
I am kneeling
all my strength is gone
Please Father don't leave me here
alone

**In Memory of a Stepfather who stepped up.
Hubie Anderson**

Time to Leave

You came for a while
And now that you are gone
How we miss your smile
God Blessed us with your presence
To change the direction of our lives
At times things were rocky and hard to bear
Now we know you were trying to show how much you care
We've been many places and seen many things
We never knew all the good things having you would bring
Knowing your pain and distress
GOD decided it was time for you to rest

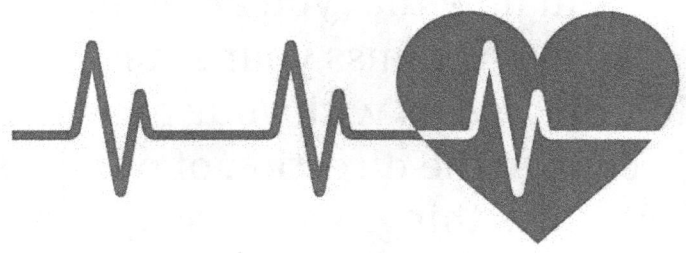

Time to Leave – Part 2

With a whisper GOD called your name
We know you are in a better place
But our lives will never be the same
So, we will keep on working
Trying to do our best
Until GOD says we have passed OUR test
At that time there will be no more to achieve
That's when GOD will say it's "Time to Leave"

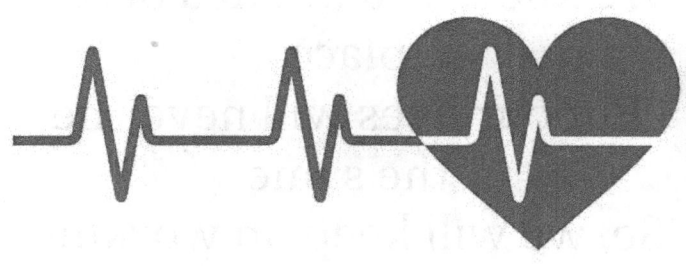

Pride

If Pride is not allowing you

To be True to YOU

Then Pride is the crutch

That is handicapping YOU

If Your Pride Allows You to Hide

Then Just know you have not yet been Freed

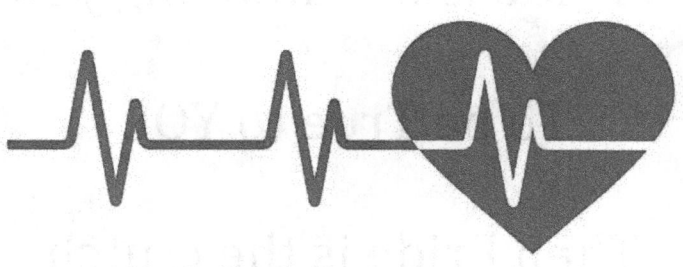

Lord Help

Lord Help me to see
Who I'm supposed to be
Help me to strive to be
A better me
Lord Help me to resist the
temptations of life
Help me to be a better husband
to my wife
Lord Help me keep Your Will first
So, I don't make my situations
worse
And if I ever feel your help I no
longer need
I pray Lord you will have mercy
on me

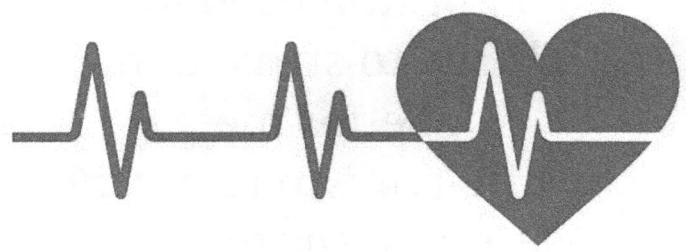

Reality

If only I could ease your mind
And tell you everything would be fine
If I could only say that one day
Everything will be ok
I would if I could in a moment
In the drop of a dime
But truly I don't have the answer
on what might happen in time
But what comes to me
Is if we never try it could
NEVER be

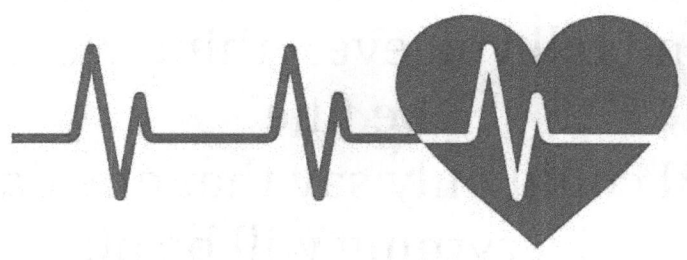

Trust

To hold it all in and refuse to share
What a heavy burden you chose to bear
Relax and Let go
And you will find a freedom
otherwise you would never know
Trust that you can say
whatever you want to say
You can share your deepest thoughts
Trust that from me you will not be judged
The things you choose to say will never be revealed
The things you choose to do will stay between me and you
Just relax Let Go and Trust

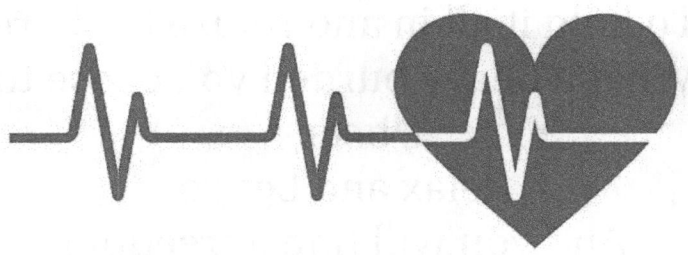

God Is

GOD is a good GOD
Through Laughter and Pain
He is always there through the sunshine and rain
When your days are cloudy and filled with despair
Just remember GOD is aware
Soon the dark clouds will roll away
And the sun will return to brighten your day
So, in time of heartache, bereavement and pain
Just remember GOD is the remedy for your Pain

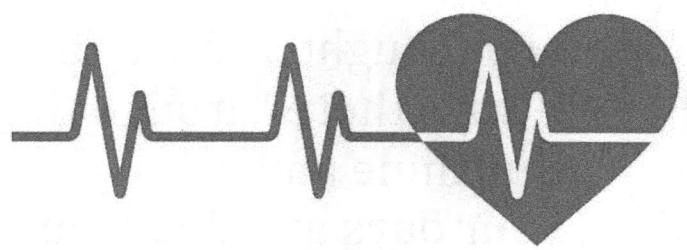

Do You Know

It's been said,
"Never let money, education,
or the beauty of a woman
Deceive you and rob you of
your blessing."

I say,
"Also beware of the words, "I
Love You"
When uttered from the same
lips that curses you."

Do You Know
Your words mean nothing
When in your actions it
doesn't show.

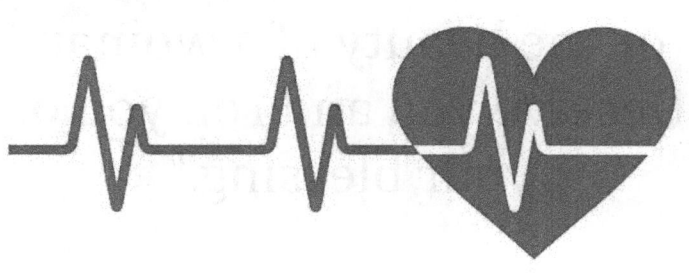

Please Lord

When my words are hurtful
and not helpful
When my hands are holding
down and not lifting up
When my actions don't
represent the
Love that my mouth speaks
Please Lord
Forgive me and hide me
in your mercy

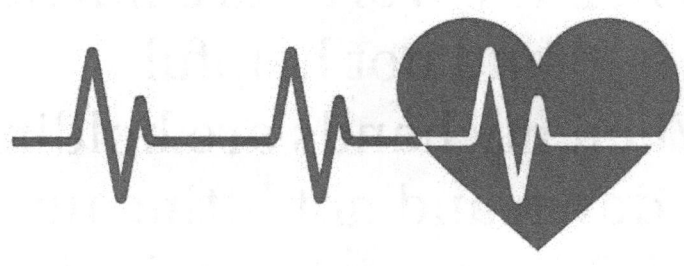

Peace

Calm my spirit as I go
through this day
Give me Peace and joy
when trials come my way
And when my Anxiety
rises
Help me to remember
with
"YOU GOD"
I can survive this

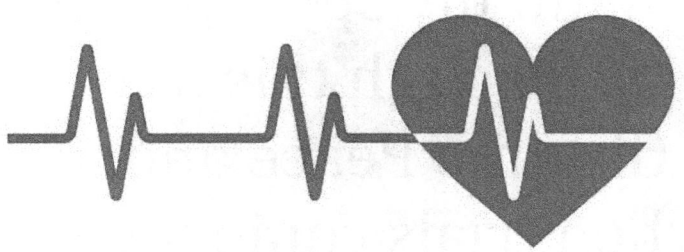

Release

Holding on to Anger
Is like an App running in
the background on your Cell phone
It slowly depletes your energy
And causes you to stop
functioning to your highest potential
So **"Force Stop"** this app from
running in your life
Unlike your cell phone, it will not
cause a slowdown
Of other operations in your life
But it will free that space for
"Forgiveness" and allow you to
operate as you were designed

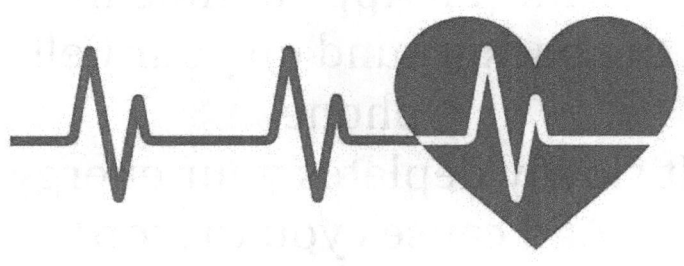

Frienemy

She has always been a friend to me
She has a special place in my heart
you see
No need to swear her to secrecy
I met this guy and he Was so in to me
Told me I was all he would ever need
Then she turned on me
Revealing all the secrets she knew
Telling him she's no good for you
Be careful the friends you keep they
will talk about you, deceive you
because their hate runs deep
Thought she was a true friend to me
But now I see she was just a
Frienemy

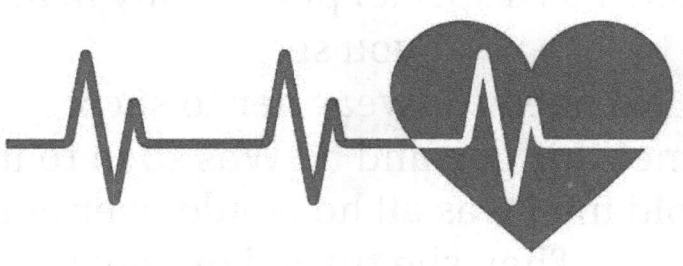

More Peace

Peace is when you have lost a loved one but memories make you smile

Being in the middle of a test, but your still able to inspire someone else with your testimony

Knowing that you are at the end of your rope
but realizing GOD has provided a safety net

That's PEACE

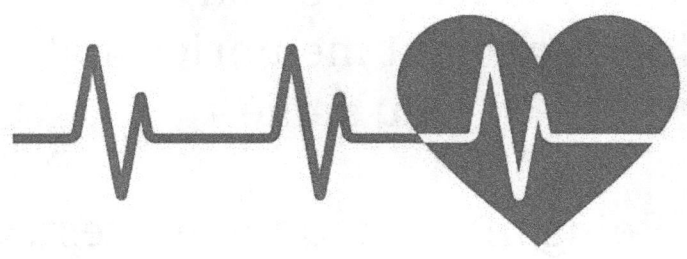

Safe

If being safe delivers its Own
portion of pain

Then in your safe place there
is not much to gain

To be safe from those who
May hurt you

Only affords you the
Opportunity to never know
their LOVE

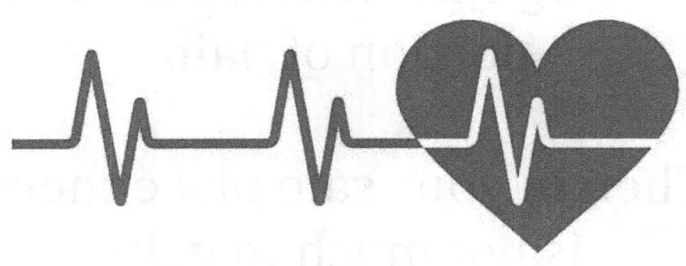

Comfortable

My heart is heavy

And my mind is busy

With the worries of life

I only wish I could break Out of this shell so I may live unbound by my fears

My chest is tight
Trying to Hold back the tears

That's when I realize I have been comfortable
Being Uncomfortable for Years

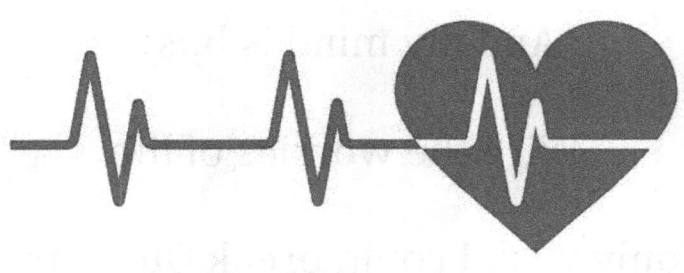

How Excellent

Your Life Is Excellent

Not because it has been perfect or without pain

But because GOD has blessed you with another day

And an opportunity to make a change

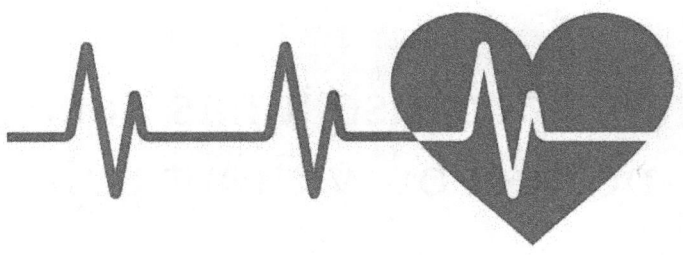

New

I hear your heart beating slow

I can feel the LOVE grows weak

Your feelings are hurt

And your Pride has been shattered

But, I had to leave before the Relationship permanently changed me

I didn't want to leave But, I couldn't stay

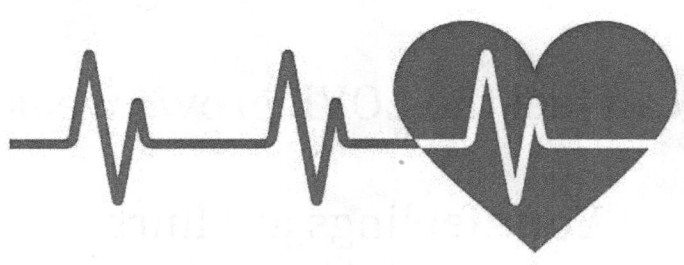

Never Settle

The same thing you settle for today
will be same thing that unsettles you
tomorrow
You see it but you settle
You Make her the center of your
attention
But she is so self –centered
She is a beauty Queen
But her personality reminds you of
an accident scene
Something you wish you had never
seen
He has a nice car But he has NO
drive
And You Settled

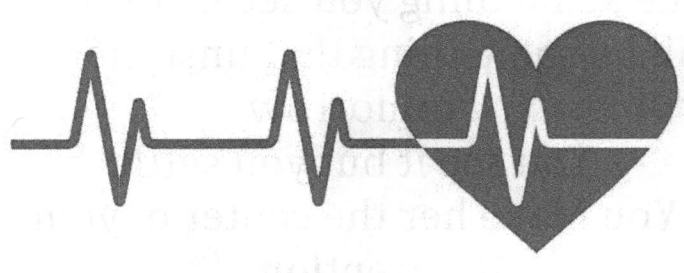

Change

If fear has you confined Blind to that which is front of you

And consumed by that which is behind you

You are in a Mental Prison

And it is up to you to make the conscious decision

Will you CHANGE

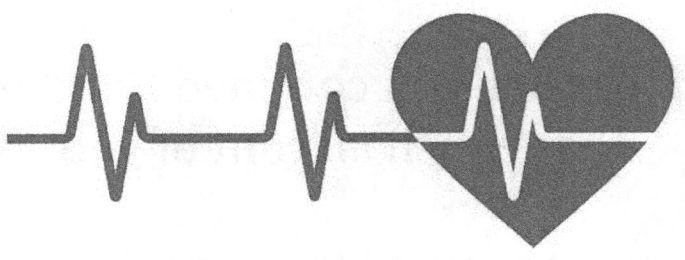

Until Next Time

In Life there are plenty of choices
and we must make those choices
everyday

Rather it be the Life we choose to
live
or the Love we choose to give

We should always remember to
pray
And when Life comes to an end
and
There is nothing left to do

When the scenes of your life
begin showing they should reflect
favorably on you

www.ingramcontent.com/pod-product-compliance
Lightning Source LLC
Chambersburg PA
CBHW051711090426
42736CB00013B/2646